To Doreen,

with love

M A Marshall

Christmas 1952

COUNTRY LIFE

# PICTURE BOOK
# OF BRITAIN

FIRST SERIES

GLAMIS CASTLE: CHILDHOOD HOME OF HER MAJESTY THE QUEEN

# COUNTRY LIFE
# PICTURE BOOK
# OF BRITAIN

## FIRST SERIES

COUNTRY LIFE LIMITED
2-10 TAVISTOCK STREET COVENT GARDEN
LONDON WC2

*First published in 1937
by Country Life Limited
Tavistock Street London W.C.2
Process engraving by
The Sun Engraving Co. Limited
London and Watford
Printed in Great Britain by
Billing and Sons Ltd
Guildford and Esher*

*Third Revised Edition
(Fifth Impression) 1951*

# LIST OF PLATES

# 1. DOVER CASTLE: THE KEY TO ENGLAND

The Constable's Tower of the great castle, guardian today, as from earliest times, of the principal entry to England from the Continent.

2. THE SEVEN SISTERS, SUSSEX

## 3. HERSTMONCEAUX CASTLE, SUSSEX

Herstmonceaux, the perfect castle of the imagination, was built of rose-red brick in the middle of the fifteenth century by Sir Roger de Fiennes, soldier and statesman.

## 4. PLUMPTON MANOR, SUSSEX

This lovely country house, lying beneath the steep northern slopes of the South Downs, stands above a sequence of three lakes connected by cascades

**5. ON THE NORTH DOWNS, NEAR WOLDINGHAM, SURREY**

A scene that evokes all the enchantment of the scented air of haytime in an English summer.

## 6. THE TOWER OF LONDON

The great fortress on Tower Hill, begun by William the Conqueror nearly 900 years ago, seen across the busy highway of the Thames.

**7. BIG BEN AND THE HOUSES OF PARLIAMENT**

A view which stands for an image of England the world over. To the right of Big Ben are the towers of Westminster Abbey.

## 8. ST JAMES'S PALACE: THE TUDOR GATEHOUSE

St James's, the principal residence of the sovereigns from 1698 to 1837, is still a royal residence and the scene of great State occasion

## 9. WESTMINSTER ABBEY

The choir of the Abbey Church of Westminster, sacred seat of the English monarchy and its people since the days of the Confessor.

10. GRAY'S INN, LONDON

## 11. SANDRINGHAM: THE KING'S COUNTRY HOME

Sandringham Hall, Norfolk, became a Royal home when it was bought in 1861 by the Prince Consort for the Prince and Princess of Wales.

**12. HAMPTON COURT, MIDDLESEX**

This part of the great royal palace (above all remembered for its associations with Wolsey) is one of Sir Christopher Wren's masterpieces of architecture.

## 13. WINDSOR CASTLE AND PARK FROM THE AIR

Windsor Castle, the oldest of the residences of the English monarchy, embodies the buildings of nearly every dynasty from the days of William the Conqueror.

## 14. THE THAMES ESTUARY, FROM HADLEIGH CASTLE, ESSEX

Of thirteenth-century Hadleigh Castle, which overlooks the estuary of the Thames near Southend, there is now little to be seen but the tumbled ruins of once mighty walls

**15. LITTLE CHART, NEAR ASHFORD, KENT**

A springtime scene with all the elements—an ancient church, a cherry orchard, a group of oast houses—that go to make an image of Kent.

**16. WILDERNESSE AVENUE, SEVENOAKS, KENT**

A study of sunlight and shadow among the trees which surround this charming Kentish town.

## 17. THE SUN INN, SAFFRON WALDEN, ESSEX

This building, dating from the fifteenth century, is remarkable for its fine seventeenth-century plaster-work, known as pargeting.

**18. ISINGTON MILL, HAMPSHIRE**

19. THE VILLAGE GREEN, WEST MILL, NEAR BUNTINGFORD, HERTFORDSHIRE

Nearby was Button Scrap, the cottage which was Charles Lamb's 'commodious mansion' in 1817.

## 20. CHEQUERS, BUCKINGHAMSHIRE

This lovely Elizabethan manor was given to the nation in 1917 by Lord Lee of Fareham for the use in perpetuity of the Prime Minister

## 21. EAST HENDRED, BERKSHIRE

A charming village, typical of the many lovely villages in this part of the country, that lies at the foot of the Berkshire Downs.

22. THE MANOR HOUSE, SUTTON COURTENAY, BERKSHIRE

## 23.  CLOVELLY,  DEVON

Clovelly, one of the most famous villages in England, owes much of its charm to its situation in a narrow, wooded rift in the cliffs of North Devon.

## 24. EAST HAGBOURNE, BERKSHIRE

East Hagbourne, with its many fine half-timbered and thatched cottages, is one of the loveliest villages in the south of England.

## 25. A BERKSHIRE LANDSCAPE

Harvest-time in the broad valley of the upper Thames near the village of Little Wittenham.

26. CODFORD ST MARY, WILTSHIRE

**27.  CLOUDS  OVER  STONEHENGE**

A study of Britain's grandest prehistoric monument which stands in majestic solitude on the southern edge of the wide expanse of Salisbury Plain.

**28. CHRISTCHURCH PRIORY, HAMPSHIRE**

The Priory, standing where the New Forest meets the sea, is the longest parish church, and one of the finest churches below cathedral rank, in England.

**29. IN THE GARDEN OF COMPTON END, NEAR WINCHESTER**

A thatched Hampshire cottage, in the middle of whose delightful garden is a massive yew of great age, trimmed to form a natural arbour.

## 30. LULWORTH COVE, DORSET

The cove is one of the most remarkable natural harbours in the country. Its circular bay is almost completely enclosed by steep cliffs.

## 31. CORFE CASTLE, DORSET

Corfe, former royal stronghold and one of the most romantic-looking ruins in the south of England, stands on an isolated hill in a gap in the long line of the Purbeck Hills.

## 32. SHAFTESBURY, DORSET

Shaftesbury, one of the most ancient towns in England, stands on a cliff-like site in the north-east of Dorset.

## 33. FINGLE BRIDGE, DEVONSHIRE

The bridge stands in a deep and wooded glen of the Teign—an ideal example of Devonshire scenery.

34. PLYMOUTH HAVEN, FROM KITS HILL, DARTMOOR

**35. POLPERRO HARBOUR, CORNWALL.**

A fishing village which owes its beauties chiefly to its situation in a steep-sided ravine on the south coast of Cornwall.

40. PORLOCK VALE, SOMERSET

**41. THE WYE AT SYMONDS YAT, HEREFORDSHIRE AND GLOUCESTERSHIRE**

The lower reaches of the Wye provide perhaps the loveliest river scenes in England; of them all none are more splendid than those to be seen from the height of Symonds Yat.

42. STOW-ON-THE-WOLD, GLOUCESTERSHIRE

## 43. LUDLOW CASTLE AND BRIDGE, SHROPSHIRE

This noble castle dates from the eleventh century and was for many years the headquarters of the Lords President of the Marches.

## 44. THE MARKET HALL, CHIPPING CAMPDEN, GLOUCESTERSHIRE

A splendid memorial of the days when this stone-built town was the capital of the Cotswolds wool-trade.

## 45. BRIDGNORTH, SHROPSHIRE

The town, which contains many picturesque half-timbered houses, lies on either side of the river gorge of the Severn.

46. WROXTON, OXFORDSHIRE

The village road at Wroxton, showing the [...]

## 47. ELY CATHEDRAL, CAMBRIDGESHIRE

The West Front of Ely Cathedral, which stands on what was once an island in the midst of fens, is among the most splendid examples of late Norman architecture in England.

**48. MAGDALEN TOWER AND BRIDGE, OXFORD**

The tower, whose chimes ring the quarters for all of Oxford, was completed in 1505. The bridge, widened in 1883, was built in 1779.

## 49. KING'S COLLEGE CHAPEL, CAMBRIDGE

King's College Chapel is the crowning achievement of fifteenth-century building.   With the College, it was founded by Henry VI in 1440.

50. IN THE CONSTABLE COUNTRY, SUFFOLK

**51. KERSEY, SUFFOLK**

One of several Suffolk villages whose prosperity in the days of the medieval wool-trade has left us a legacy of noble churches and harmonious domestic architecture.

52. HEYBRIDGE MILL, ESSEX

**53. HEMINGFORD GREY, HUNTINGDONSHIRE**

The little village of Hemingford Grey (or East Hemingford) lies between Huntingdon and St Ives on the River Ouse not far from where it reaches the Fens.

## 54. SALISBURY CATHEDRAL, WILTSHIRE

The spire of one of England's most glorious Gothic cathedrals seen from a garden in the Close.

## 55. NORWICH CATHEDRAL, NORFOLK

The cathedral church, in this 'city of churches', was founded in 1096. The tower is a noble example of late Norman architecture.

## 56. WORCESTER CATHEDRAL

The cathedral stands above the quiet waters of the Severn, its tower a splendid memorial of the latter half of the fourteenth century

## 57.  WELLS  CATHEDRAL,  SOMERSET

The statues on the great West Front form the finest gallery of medieval sculpture in England.

## 58. LEVENS HALL, WESTMORLAND

An Elizabethan country house, as interesting for its interior decoration as it is famous for the topiary work of its gardens.

### 59. COMPTON WYNYATES, WARWICKSHIRE

Compton Wynyates, built largely of a lovely rosy brick, is perhaps the best known of the Tudor mansions in England.

## 60. FOUNTAINS ABBEY, YORKSHIRE

The ruins of the Chapel of the Nine Altars in the grandest and best preserved of the Cistercian houses in England, founded in 1132.

## 61. STONEGATE, YORK

A street of ancient houses leading to the Minster, in a city which was the capital of the Roman province of Britain.

**62. IN SILEX BAY, NEAR FLAMBOROUGH, YORKSHIRE**

A scene typical of the sheer chalk cliffs of this stretch of the Yorkshire coast, which run the length of the peninsula which is

**63. HADDON HALL, DERBYSHIRE**

The ascent to the gate-tower of a great medieval home, the creation of generations of builders between the twelfth and seventeenth centuries.

64. PEVERIL CASTLE, DERBYSHIRE

**65. THE PEAK, FROM RUSHUP EDGE, DERBYSHIRE**

The view across the Vale of Edale from the great whaleback ridge of Rushup Edge.

## 66. LITTLE MORETON HALL, CHESHIRE

One of the most picturesque and best-preserved 'black and white' Tudor manor houses of Cheshire.

## 67. CARDINGMILL VALLEY, SHROPSHIRE

The view to the old town of Church Stretton down a wooded valley on the east side of The Long Mynd.

## 68. IN THE VALE OF EVESHAM, WORCESTERSHIRE

The happy village of Childs Wickham: a captivating scene in the lovely fruit-growing and market-garden country of the Avon valley.

**69. MALVERN, FROM NORTH HILL, WORCESTERSHIRE**

The hills of Malvern stand out above the wide plain of the Severn, and are a landmark from both the Cotswolds and the Welsh hills.

**70. GREAT GABLE AND STY HEAD TARN, CUMBERLAND**

The shapely mass of Great Gable dominates the head of Wasdale. It is a peak loved by walkers and and rock-climbers alike, for both may find their ways to its summit.

## 71. KESWICK AND DERWENTWATER, CUMBERLAND

Keswick is in the northern part of the Lake District in the beautiful valley of the Greta, with Skiddaw on the north and Derwentwater, beloved of the Lake Poets, to the south.

## 72. DERWENTWATER IN WINTER

The still beauty of a winter's day over a lake which is held to be the loveliest stretch of water in England.

## 73. HONISTER PASS, CUMBERLAND

The pass, at its highest point 1190 feet above sea-level, runs from Borrowdale to Buttermere, here seen in the far distance.

74. UPPER BORROWDALE, CUMBERLAND

## 75.  IN THE CHEVIOT HILLS, NORTHUMBERLAND

A view of the wild border country, looking up the valley of Harthope Burn to the Cheviot beyond.

76. NEAR MIDDLETON-IN-TEESDALE, CO. DURHAM

## 77. DURHAM CATHEDRAL

The supreme example of Norman architecture in England, begun in 1093 on a steep cliff overhanging the River Wear.

### 78. PUFFINS ON SKOMER ISLE

Skomer is a windswept island off the coast of Pembrokeshire where puffins have their home.

## 79. HARVEST NEAR BALA, IN MERIONETHSHIRE

A peaceful valley-scene in this glorious countryside, whose lake is the largest natural sheet of water in Wales.

## 80. PORTMEIRION, NORTH WALES

A village on the Tremadoc estuary, created by its architect-owner, Mr Clough Williams-Ellis, in the style of a Dalmatian resort.

## 81.  MIRROR OF SNOWDON

The view of the peaks of the Snowdon group from the Capel Lakes provides the most majestic mountain landscape in Britain.

82. MENAI STRAITS AND SUSPENSION BRIDGE

## 83. ON THE NITH ESTUARY, SOLWAY FIRTH

Solway Firth, which lies between Scotland and the English county of Cumberland, is famous for the rapid rising and falling of its tides.

**84. THE PALACE OF HOLYROODHOUSE, EDINBURGH**

Holyrood, first built in the reign of James IV of Scotland, is still used as the residence of our kings and queens when they visit the northern capital

**85. THE TWEED AT OLD MELROSE**

In the country which will for ever be associated with Sir Walter Scott.

86. IN THE PASS OF GLENCOE

## 87. LOCH LOCHY, INVERNESS-SHIRE

Loch Lochy forms, with Loch Linnhe and Loch Ness, a great part of the length of the Caledonian Canal.

**88. ON THE ROAD TO INCHNADAMPH, SUTHERLAND**

The hamlet of Inchnadamph lies at the south-eastern end of Loch Assynt, which is dominated to the north by the massive height of Quinag.

**89. LOCH BROOM, ROSS AND CROMARTY**

Loch Broom, at the mouth of which is Ullapool, runs far into West Ross. In the distance, veiled in mist, are the heights of Frannich Forest, and on the left Ben Derg.

90. LOCH CAIRNBAWN, SUTHERLANDSHIRE

Great works of art or craftsmanship
give to the world standards by which it may acquire
a true sense of values.

# ROLLS-ROYCE

## THE BEST CAR IN THE WORLD

# This England . . .

*Lose Hill, Derbyshire*

WHEN FEW COULD READ and fewer write, men would affix to the record of their declarations or commands a seal—that all might recognise by this sign or picture whence came the document, and its true authority. And when it ceased to be valid—as at death or at the beginning of a reign—the matrix was publicly destroyed. But many lovely seals of the old English corporations are preserved to us and in some sort illustrate the old legal maxim that corporations never die. Thus do we still say that men have " set the seal of approval " upon a thing—as, for example the beer of Bass or Worthington. Indeed a fair example this, for here are beers brewed with traditional skill by an old English corporation—that surely will not die while England lives.

ISSUED BY BASS AND WORTHINGTON, BURTON-UPON-TRENT, ENGLAND

# FOR FACES & PLACES

# ILFORD
## SELOCHROME
# FILMS